HOW TO BECOME
DEBT FREE

By

Ricky Corum

Copyright © 2021 Ricky Corum
All rights reserved.
ISBN-9798759098256

BOOKS BY RICKY CORUM

FICTION

Murder at the Heights

Murder on Military Road

The Bicycle Gang

The Lipstick Murders

NON-FICTION

How to Become Debt Free

How to Be Your Own Contractor

DEDICATION

This book is dedicated to my son Damion, who inspired me to write it. And to all readers who dare to dream of living debt free and gaining their financial freedom.

The ideas, and concepts in this book are my opinion based on what has worked for me on my path to financial freedom. It may or may not work for you; I cannot possibly know the full details of any reader's personal situation or needs.

With regards to accounting or tax matters, the author and publisher strongly suggest that the reader seek, when necessary, the services of appropriate licensed professionals and comply with the local licensing requirements of the community in which the reader resides or conducts business.

Neither the publisher nor the author intends, with this publication, to render legal or accounting service or advice. The author and publisher disclaim any personal liability, loss or risk incurred because of the use of this application, either directly or indirectly, of any advice, information or methods presented herein.

INTRODUCTION

I author this book with the hope that it will provide you a simple path to becoming debt free and gaining your financial freedom.

I was raised in a large family of ten, there were eight children, four boys and four girls. We were poor, I didn't understand just how poor until I was about ten years old. My mother and father worked hard, but it was a constant struggle just to pay the bills. My parents provided us with the basics, like food, shelter, but all my clothes were hand-me-downs from my two older brothers.

After high school I join the Army and spent two and half years in Germany. When I got out of the Army, I started working construction and worked my way from a laborer to apprentice brick mason, and later a mason. I then became a superintendent for a large general contractor.

In 1986 after a downturn in the economy my company kick me to the curb. I'd been working there for over three years, and a year earlier the company had given me an all-expenses paid vacation to Antigua, a reward for making my yearly quotas. It was the best job I'd ever had, we had a wonderful team, great leadership, great fun, and I made good money. In fact, it was the first construction job I ever had, that actually paid benefits. But a year later I was without a job and without a future. That's when I realized how poor and vulnerable my family and I really were.

I once heard the Author of "Rich Dad Poor Dad" Robert T. Kiyosaki say that "the poor and middle-class work for money, and the rich have money work for them." At the time I didn't really understand what he meant by that statement.

I was like most people who never study how to manage their

money. I knew in my own life, that if things were going to change, first I had to change. I had to realize that I was the problem, so I had to grow wiser, and learn how to manage my money.

I needed to learn to put my money to work for me and enjoy the tax benefits of generating income that doesn't come from a paycheck. Buying or building assets that deliver cash flow is putting your money to work for you.

It's not how much money you earn, it's how much money you keep. If you want to be rich, you need to be financially informed. Today, we need greater financial intelligence to simply survive. Part of that survival is leaning to invest. Investing only takes a few dollars to start and grow into something big. Your assets need to become large enough to grow by themselves.

Accounting is the most confusing, boring subject in the world, but if you want to get rich long-term, it is the most important subject. You must understand the difference between and asset and a liability and buy assets. The most important thing you need to know is, an asset puts money in your pocket and a liability takes money out of your pocket.

CHAPTER 1

UNDERSTANDING FINANCIAL FREEDOM

The key to financial freedom and great wealth is a person's ability to convert earned income into passive and/or portfolio income. Ordinary earned income is money you work for, and passive and portfolio income is money working for you. Spend less than you earn, invest the surplus, avoid debt. Do this and you'll end up rich.

There are many things that money can buy, but the most valuable of all is your Financial Freedom. Money is a form of power, but what is even more powerful is your financial freedom and education. Money comes and goes, but if you have the education about how money works, you gain power over it and can began building your wealth. Most people went to school and never learned how money works, so they spend their lives working for money.

This book is all about a proven path to your financial freedom. This strategy is not meant to be answers, but something that will assist you to get out of debt and grow wealthier, no matter what happens in a world of change and uncertainty.

The definition of financial freedom is to not be reliant on anyone and living debt free. When living debt free, you will be completely independent of a job, lender, or any type of government support.

This book is written with the belief that the ideal situation is to have no bills and a substantial income in retirement. Wouldn't it be great to achieve, a situation where you own your own home, your cars, have no installment debt, and enough investments to live off the interest for the rest of your life.

To achieve this goal, you will need to follow a debt free strategy. It's impossible to reach financial freedom doing things the way we've been taught in the past. You need to understand how we've been misled, then you need to design an efficient strategy, to use the money you are currently earning to reach your goals.

These ideas are counter to traditional wisdom, but traditional wisdom is incorrect. It's incorrect, because it's wisdom that is promoted by the businesses that profit from doing what's good for them, and not what's good for you. Our economy is designed to make you work all your life, to accumulate wealth for the companies you do business with, not for yourself.

The most overwhelming example of this is a home mortgage. When it comes to houses, most people work all their lives paying for a home they never actually own. In other words, most people buy a new house every few years, each time incurring a new 30-year loan to pay off the previous one.

If you buy a home with a 30-year conventional mortgage, you will pay for that loan three times. That means that two-thirds of the mortgage is interest. Interest is the profit the mortgage company makes for lending you the money.

As an example, if you buy a home for $250,000, with a $50,000 down payment and a $200,000 mortgage, you will end up paying $600,000 or more over the life of a 30-year loan. This means that you will pay at least four hundred thousand dollars in interest. So, you will have to earn an extra four hundred thousand dollars, to help make the mortgage companies rich.

You'll need to craft a debt free strategy that will keep the wealth you produce for yourself. The power of keeping and investing the money you waste on mortgage interest alone could change your life. We're not talking about earning extra money here, these four hundred thousand dollars is money you are going to need to earn anyway. The debt free strategy just gives you control of who ends up with it, you, or the mortgage company.

After a home mortgage, another form of legal theft is auto loans. Banks and finance companies are willing to give you up to five or six years to pay off a car loan. That's because the loan is like a mini home mortgage, only the interest rate is higher.

Insurance is another rip off, when it comes to insurance, most people have little or no understanding of the value of what they're buying. Insurance companies don't lose money on Insurance Policies! Some of them go out of business after making bad investments, but they don't lose anything on their insurance programs. There may be a small number of people who pay a few dollars in premiums and end up making a large claim. In that case it might appear that an insurance company has a loss, but they have thousands of other people paying premiums each month to cover the benefits that they pay out.

When an insurance company sells you a policy, they are gambling that you are one of the fortunate ones who cost them nothing and pay them thousands over the years! They have statistically calculated that you will never file a claim.

Some of the financial "methods" we are taught, or just pick up are wrong! They can prevent us from ever-achieving real financial freedom.

Two of those methods are *"Saving money, a little at a time, as you go through life,"* and *"You need to use credit to develop and maintain a good credit rating."*

When you receive financial advice, it usually includes instructions on how to save money, as you work your way though life. Many "financial advisors" tell you to save 10% of your income as an investment for the future. This is not bad advice, it's just the way it's most often applied that causes people to move slowly toward their goal of financial freedom, instead of taking the fastest route.

Efficiency comes from focusing on one task at a time. The debt free strategy is the fastest, and safest route to your financial goals. You will first eliminate all debt, then you will start to save.

You'll get to a point where you won't care what your credit rating is, because you won't need it anymore. Most people are never taught, by family or by our education system, how to manage their income. So, they become the students of advertisers and the money-lending companies behind them.

You're told by the media what kind of car you should be driving to look successful? You are told what kind of house you should live in to be happy, or what kind of clothes will make you socially acceptable? A bigger home or faster car won't make you near as happy as the absence of the pressures of making those monthly mortgage payments.

With the debt free strategy, you can be driving an acceptable car and living in a lovely home, but you will have no payments to make on anything but food, heat, and the minimum legal taxes. At that point you will be protected from layoffs, and economic downturns. You will be in a place that few people ever achieve because they are continually misled to waste their wealth.

CHAPTER 2

TAKE CONTROL OF YOUR MONEY

Once you figure out how much money you were spending on interest by using credit cards, financing cars for 4 to 6 years, and paying out a 30-year mortgage, you will be furious. But when you see what that same money can do for you once it is redirected in a way that the compound interest works for you, you'll be astonished.

When I worked out my debt free elimination and wealth-building plan, I realized that the same money I was spending every month could pay off the same house we were currently paying for, plus earn us thousands of dollars in investments.

I began researching these methods because, I believed that, *if I didn't hit the lottery to make me hundreds of thousands of dollars, I would have to keep working until the day I died.*

I was making good money, but no matter how much I earned, we we're barely getting by. We had nice TVs and newer cars, but we were living from month to month. In fact, we were worse off than when I had made less money, because now we had larger payments and bigger balances on everything.

I realized that I needed to continue bringing in a higher income just to pay the bills, just to hang on to what we had, and nothing was building for the future. I knew, I had to continue this high-income level at all costs, or I would be in real trouble. I was feeling vulnerable to the economy, to my employer, to anything that could upset my income stream. That's when I discovered that there really was a way to achieve financial freedom, a way that didn't require a bunch of extra money, it was simply a method of redirecting the money I was already making.

The Debt Free system could not only get me out of debt but

could also make me rich. For the first time I felt like I really had a chance to live out the kind of future I had only dream about. I also realized that a side benefit of the strategy was that I would never need credit again. In fact, in most situations, people using cash can live better than people operating on credit.

Money Talks? It really does when it's real money. If you have the money, you can often strike bargains that aren't available to the credit addict. I bought a car, from a dealer, it was used but in like-new condition and I got a decent price because I stood in the dealership with my checkbook. I tapped the checkbook on the salesman's desk and said, *"I'm going to write a check to buy a car today. I can write the check here, or I can walk across the street and write a check at the dealer over there. You decide."* They decided not to let me get out the door, and I drove away in a wonderful car.

Someone interested in that same car, but asking for bank financing, would have had no bargaining leverage, so they would have paid the full asking price. Then they would have been taken to the cleaners with the finance charges and ended up paying thousands more than I did for the same car.

Cash is king! Even when it comes to buying homes. You can visit the sheriff's tax sales in your county and often buy homes for pennies on the dollar. Some of these houses are incredible values. You would be amazed at what you can buy at these sales if you have cash. You could easily furnish a home, buy a car, buy a boat, or anything else you can imagine. But it all goes to the person with the cash.

When you're in debt, you are forced to live like you have a lower income, because when you bought something on credit in the past, you have committed a portion of your current income. If eighty percent of your after-tax income goes to credit debt payments, those purchases from the past are forcing you to live on twenty percent of your current income which lowers your standard of living. Eighty percent may sound like a lot, but if you add up your credit card interest with your car loans, and mortgage interest you should get there.

Someone who is completely debt-free, and making the same

income as you, has that eighty percent to spend or invest. They get to live on 100% of their income simply because they operate on a cash basis. However, before you can get to operating on a cash basis, you will need to move through the bill and mortgage elimination steps.

There are some obstacles to watch out for. The obstacles that helped you get into the dilemma you are in today. First there's the Monthly Payment Trap.

Our monetary system has trained us to think in terms of monthly payments. When we go to buy a TV set, or a car, or even a home, we think in terms of how much we can afford to pay each month. In fact, I've purchase cars where the salesperson asked me "how much do you think you can swing each month."

We never think about the actual cost of the purchase. Will it be good for us? Are we getting ripped off? Is it ridiculous to pay 21% interest on a TV, or to pay three times for our home over the life of a 30-year mortgage?

The reason we never think beyond the monthly payment is because, *"Everyone's doing it, so it must be the right thing to do. Everyone pays 30 years for a house, don't they? How else could anyone ever afford one?"*

We go out to buy something and the only two numbers we consider are our monthly income and the total monthly expenses. Or we look at a credit card to see how much room there is before we go over the limit. Whatever's left, is spendable credit! It is like we consider it our duty to keep our monthly payments equal to our monthly income. We have been trained to look at the wrong part of the equation. It does matter how much the total cost is! It will have a serious effect on your future wealth.

Every penny of interest you pay is money you must earn, money that should be contributing to your wealth, but instead you are donating it to the wealth-building of a bank or finance company. You're only going to be able to create a certain amount of wealth in your lifetime, and you can't afford to waste any of that wealth-creation power to make other people rich. You need to keep as much of it as possible for yourself!

I know now that using financing has been damaging both to

my short-term and my long-term financial interests. Credit sucks! Except for buying your first home, you don't ever want to use credit for anything. Credit is wicked, and I've seen debt crush people, ruin marriages, destroy healthy minds and bodies.

CHAPTER 3

DEBT MANAGEMENT PLAN

When I discovered this simple path to wealth, I was shocked after working out the numbers. Bills which I had been paying the minimum payment, month after month for years, were eliminated in less than a year! After my bills were paid off, I was able to more than double my mortgage payment.

I had a 30-year mortgage and planned to pay it off just like everyone else. I knew about mortgage reduction plans, but never really thought seriously about using one, because I could never find the extra money required. Even a reduction to 15 or 20 years seemed like forever.

With this strategy, I found the extra money by paying off all my charge accounts first. Then, using the same money I had been paying on credit cards and car loans each month, I was able to accelerate the payoff of my home to just over 7 years. And this was accomplished with the same income stream I already had. It didn't require any additional income to make it work.

If I had continued using my income the way most people do, I would have eventually paid off the house and saved a little money. But it would have taken me 30 years, and I would have paid hundreds of thousands of dollars to the mortgage company in interest payments.

For this strategy to work, you will need to concentrate your finances on one thing at a time. So, begin by paying off all your bills, because you don't want to weaken the calculations by trying to save now.

Consider the interest on both the bill-payoff and the savings sides of the equation. If you are putting money into a savings or money market account at, say 4% or 5% interest, and you are concurrently paying 20% on credit interest, you are moving backwards at a rate of 11% to 15% a year. And when you compound that over several years, it becomes an astounding loss of your income.

If you use a dollar to pay off a bill where you are being charged 20% interest, you are making more on your money than if you put it in an investment where you are earning a much lower rate.

Every dollar you put into savings or investments, instead of bill payoff, is earning you less of a return than it could be. So, you do not want to invest until after you have no credit debt.

The interest rate is lower on your mortgage than credit cards levels, but you are still getting an above-average return on your money by using it to pay off the mortgage. This is because, you must compare the return you receive by prepaying your mortgage.

The goal is to make you debt free in the shortest possible time. And nothing helps you feel better than knowing you no longer have a mortgage payment. When you own your home, you are protected from potential downsizings, inflation and decreases in the economy.

The total money makeover debt free strategy that I'm proposing is not based on expectations, but on mathematics. It is founded on the principle that you want to become debt-free as soon as possible and start building wealth for your future.

Compound interest is powerful, and right now it is probable stacked against you. To achieve financial freedom, you must learn to manage compound interest in your life. The debt free strategy is based on a mathematical process that will short out the compound interest working against you. It then shows you how to turn your income around so you can later maximize the power of compound interest to work for you.

You must also protect yourself from the bad things that could happen to you. This means that you'll need to have insurance to protect you from a catastrophic event. It is more cost-effective to assume the risk of insuring yourself from life's minor illnesses, by maximizing the deductibles on your policies. That is much cheaper than paying an insurance company a higher premium, month after month, to cover those minor costs.

Once you follow these strategies and recommendations, you could have the resources to protect yourself from everything you are currently buying insurance for, and you will need little or no insurance other than for personal liability.

There are four steps in the debt management plan to achieve your financial freedom:

Step 1. Finding a Rocket booster
Step 2. Paying off debt
Step 3. Operate on a cash basis
Step 4. Began building your wealth

By following these steps, you can achieve real financial freedom in just a few years, and you will never need to use credit again. Most people who follow these strategies can be completely debt-free, including their home mortgage, in 4 to 7 years. And then they can begin to build retirement wealth with all the money they had previously been wasting on debt payments.

How much better off are you going to be 6 or 7 years from now, it's up to you, are you willing to try an innovative approach or are you going to continue down the same old path, you've been on?

CHAPTER 4

FINDING YOUR ROCKET BOOSTER

The first step in applying the Debt Free Strategy is to find your initial *"Rocket Booster."* This is the money that will drive your debt payoff pump. It is buried in your current monthly expenses, and in your savings opportunities.

The *Rocket Booster* doesn't have to be a lot of money. The amount you are shooting for in a *Rocket Booster* is 10% of your net, monthly income. In other words, if you bring home $2,000 a month, you are trying to put together a $200 *Rocket Booster*. If you can afford more, do it. This is not a game; your goal is to pay off all your debts, in the shortest amount of time.

Reduce your spending to the minimum. Consider diverse ways to try and trim your expenses. This allows you to put more money into the payoff process. Look for ways to reduce your food and entertainment expenses. And ways to save money when you are buying clothes and household requirements.

Let's suppose that you have just received a three percent cost of living raise. Great, now you can take a portion of it, say one percent, and use it as part of your Rocket Booster. Next year when you get another raise you do the same thing, after a couple of years you're talking about real money, and your income is still increasing by two percent a year at the same time.

Everyone has hidden savings opportunities included in their monthly expenditures. You can blow a lot of money the way you buy your car(s), your home, and your insurance. These items offer the highest monthly potential for finding your hidden *Rocket*

Booster.

Buying a new car is simply throwing thousands of dollars away. You can buy a two-year-old car that is in "Like-New" condition. A new car loses half its value in the first two years. Let the person who bought the new car take the 50% depreciation on the car, not you. Also, never take more than 36 months financing on a car. People who take longer loans always owe more than the car is worth.

Never buy any after-market products or services from a car dealer.

Cars come from the factory with rust protection, so don't get talked into buying undercoating. And if you see anything on the sticker like, "Market Adjustment" that's a secret name for additional profit for the dealer. Don't pay any "Documentation Fees." This is a dealer charging you for his people to do the paperwork on your purchase. The dealer should also pay shipping, freight, delivery, or "Prep" charges, not you.

Don't take any Extended Warranties of any kind. Like most other forms of insurance, warranty policies are never likely to be needed. I used to buy extended warranties on everything I purchased, but one day I realized that I had never made a claim on one. With the savings I have realized since, I can afford to fix any of the once-covered products that might break. Cancel all extended warranties and get refunds for the unused time on them.

Life insurance is to assure your family of a continuance of your income stream, should you stop producing it yourself. What you want to do is buy pure "Term" life insurance, with a sufficient death benefit that would generate your present monthly income if it were invested in a good mutual fund. You should then put together a Trust (your lawyer can help) for the beneficiary of your life insurance. The trust will invest the money from your insurance policy and pay your survivors the monthly interest as a continuation of your income stream.

Do not consider any kind of insurance that supposedly, builds a cash value or contains an investment program along with the life benefit. "Whole life" or any other type of "Cash Value" life insurance is one of the biggest rip-offs out there. Most people don't know this, but the cash value that you build up in a whole life policy over the years belongs to the insurance company not to you or your beneficiaries! They sell it to you like you are building up an investment, but if you want to touch any of the "cash" you must borrow it and pay it back with interest. And when you die, they don't pay your survivors the policy's death benefit, plus the cash value you have built up. They just pay the death benefit and keep the cash value.

The reason they sell "Cash Value," or other "Investment" types of life insurance is because they are commission rich policies to sell. They don't make as much commission on selling Term insurance.

All types of "Cash Value" or "Universal Life" policies are bad for your wealth building. You can do much better by buying the best value term policy for the coverage you really need and investing the rest into your debt-elimination and wealth-building plan.

It's the same with automobile insurance. If you accept all the coverages your insurance agent starts suggesting, you will end up paying hundreds of dollars a year more than you need to. Insurance companies have many shrewd ways of making you pay twice for the same types of coverage. For example, "Uninsured and Under-insured Motorist" coverage. This is your insurance company getting you to pay premiums for coverage you are already paying for under the "Medical" section of your policy.

In an insurance's company's car policy booklet under the description for Uninsured Motor Vehicle – Coverage U: "We will pay damages for *bodily injury* an insured is legally entitled to collect. "Now in the same booklet under Medical Expenses Coverage C: "We will pay reasonable medical expenses, for *bodily injury* caused by accident. Sounds familiar, doesn't it? It seems that your "Medical" coverage would suffice. Asking you to pay a separate premium to cover the same *bodily injury* expenses, simply because those injuries are the fault of an uninsured or underinsured motorist, is putting a double burden on you. Many states mandate

Uninsured Motorist and Underinsured Motorist minimum coverages, make sure that you obey these laws

These are a few suggestions of areas where you may be paying more each month than you need to. And every dollar you are wasting on these excess expenditures is a dollar that is not currently free to be included in your *Rocket Booster*.

Once you see how much just a few extra *Rocket Booster* dollars can speed up your debt elimination plan, you will become as diligent as I am to find every penny. Look at every expense area you have. Are you really using all the premium (extra charge) Cable TV channels you are currently paying for each month? Could you brown bag it to lunch more often? Do you pay someone to cut the grass or shovel the snow when you could do it yourself? Are you paying full prices for all your groceries when your weekly newspaper is stuffed with discount coupons?

We also waste money on appearances when we try to keep up with our neighbors, but our neighbors may be going bankrupt.

Everything they have they bought on credit, and if they lost their income, they would possibly be homeless in a month or two. They are living an illusion, and you will be too if you try to compete with them. Forget trying to impress people with your possessions. Wait until you retired early, then they will really be impressed!

Some people choose to leave the fast-paced, high-pressure lifestyles for a more relaxed, less-expensive, and safer small-town life. This doesn't mean, living off the land, or living like a recluse. I'm just suggesting that there is money you are spending each month that could get you out of debt faster. If it's worth it to you to become truly debt-free, you can find it. Examine your life ruthlessly, to see where you are wasting your money and eliminate those wastes. You will be able to find your *Rocket Booster* from this examination alone.

CHAPTER 5

PAYING OFF DEBT

Before you pay off, you're bills, you must make sure that you cannot create any more. Cut up and throw away all your credit cards, except for travel cards that cannot carry a balance (like *American Express*) and gasoline cards for road emergencies when you do not have cash with you. There is no reason for keeping credit cards, none. Give up the Plastic!

You might say to yourself, *"What if an emergency comes up"* or *"I just use them during the month, then pay them off as soon as the bill comes in."* Using a credit card, even with the intention of paying them off when the bill arrives, causes people to purchase more than they would if they were writing a check or laying down cash. The plastic is painless, and too convenient for impulse buying and impulse buying hurts your financial health.

For our purposes, a "Bill" is a debt that can be completely paid off. Ongoing costs such as utilities are "Expenses," and they are not to be included in your debt-elimination plan, because they are never totally paid off.

The first thing you need to do is get a copy of all your bills together. Write down each account's total balance and its corresponding required monthly payment on the *Bill Payoff Order* form in Appendix A. When you have all the bills written down, divide the "Total Balance" amounts by their respective *"Monthly Payments* and put the answers in column 4."

For example, let's say you have a Visa card with a $500 balance, and a minimum monthly payment of $25. You would divide $500 by $25 and get the answer of twenty. This is the first step in determining the proper order in which to pay off your bills.

Then, starting with the lowest division answer, number the bills from "1" to whatever number of bills you need to pay off. Put these answers in the "*Pay off Priority*" column five.

If you had two bills (the Visa above and a department store charge).

The Visa division gave you the answer of twenty, while the department store came out at seventeen, the department store account would be number "1" and the Visa account number "2". These numbers will indicate the order in which you should pay off your bills.

It doesn't matter which account has the highest interest rate, because this system will accelerate your bill payoff to the point that you won't be paying enough months of interest for it to make a difference. You're going to beat the banks at the interest game, and the mathematics will begin to work in your favor.

Add your "*Rocket Booster*" that you've accumulated to the regular payment for bill number "1" each month until the bill is completely paid off. If you put together a $200 *Rocket Booster* and added it to the Visa account we talked about above, you would completely pay the bill off in just over two months! Just think, a bill that you would normally be paying down for years could be gone in just over two months. Even if you could only add a $100 *Rocket Booster*, the Visa bill would be completely paid off in four months.

After bill number 1 is paid off, the next month you take all of what you had been paying on the Visa account, the $200 *Rocket Booster* plus the $25 normal Visa payment, and you add all of it ($225) to the regular payment of bill number "2". If that bill had a monthly payment of say $50, you would be paying a total of $275 each month on that bill. It too would be gone in a few months, and you would then be adding the full $275 to the payment of bill number 3, and so on through all your consumer credit bills. By the time you get to bigger bills, like your car payment, your *Rocket Booster* will have grown to an impressive amount.

Once you have knocked off all the regular revolving credit

accounts, including any car payments, you'll be ready for the big one, the mortgage payment. In some cases, people have eliminated all their debt except their mortgage by the end of the first year on the Debt Free strategy. At this point they will often have a *Rocket Booster* that is equal to their mortgage payment, sometimes as much as twice their mortgage payment.

Don't be demoralized if it takes you a little longer to get through the bills that precede your mortgage.

Many people take longer than a year to get to the mortgage and still end up debt-free in a total of between 5 to 7 years. That still beats paying a mortgage for over 30 years and will save you thousands of dollars.

Adding your now-large *Rocket Booster* to your mortgage, you'll begin knocking off the principal at an unbelievable rate. Your equity in your home will skyrocket, for two reasons. Number one, 100% of your *Rocket Booster* is reducing your principal balance (adding to your equity, the portion of the house you own). Number two, the portion of your regular monthly payment that is interest will be falling dramatically, because it is calculated each month on the "remaining unpaid balance."

Since your *Rocket Booster* is pounding down the unpaid balance, the interest calculation will be performed each month on a smaller and smaller balance amount. So more of your regular monthly payment amount will also be applied to the unpaid balance, further accelerating the payoff process. You should contact your mortgage company directly and ask for specific instructions on how to make additional principal prepayments along with your regular monthly payment.

If you are not making a mortgage payment on a house, you will use the first step to pay off your revolving credit debt (bank cards, store charge cards, gas cards with any balance on them, car loans, and so on). Then you will put all the monthly money you have freed up by paying off your bills into moderate-to low-risk investments, to build up a down-payment on your home. Then, as soon as you get into your new house, you will start the process of paying off the mortgage!

I know this may sound a little crazy, but I recommend that you do not save any money until all debt is gone. You will achieve a lot more, a lot faster, by focusing your total available income on bill payoff, than you will by spreading it thin and trying to save simultaneously. If you want to put a thousand dollars or so into the bank as an emergency backup fund that's fine, but you should get all your available income paying off bills as soon as possible.

Let's say that you currently need $4,000 net income each month to cover your bills and expenses.

Let's also say that you can put together a rocket booster of $400, ten percent of your monthly income. If you want to build up a six-month cash reserve before you start eliminating debts, then you need to save six times $4,000 (your monthly requirement), or $24,000 to give you six month's-worth of cash. If you divide the $400 you have available each month into the $24,000 cash reserve amount you plan to save up, it will take you 60 months or five full years just to build a cash reserve, before you start eliminating your debt. If you follow the debt free strategy to the letter, you could be completely debt free in those same five years by paying off all debt first and saving second!

But you have now changed the situation, after you have paid off your mortgage, car payment and other credit payments, you could get along on just $1,000 a month. That would mean that you would only need $6,000 (instead of $24,000) for your six-month emergency fund. And, you would now have about $3,000 a month to put away (because you have no bills to pay), so it would take you only two months to save up your six-month emergency money instead of five years!

For this step of the strategy, concentrate all available money into the bill pay off process. This doesn't mean that you can't ever go to a show or out to dinner, but it does mean that there are trade-offs. If you go out to dinner, that could mean adding a month on the payoff timeline for a bill, delaying, the day you become debt free. However, I recommend that you do not shut off all forms of entertainment, because you will get annoyed and give up on your road to financial freedom.

This debt free strategy will work, but the most important feature is your commitment. Only your commitment will keep you on course, I can't make you follow the plan. When you put this system to work, it won't be terribly hard, but it will be challenging.

When you start paying off your debt, any time you feel yourself beginning to waver, remember, the huge amount of debt you are carrying now will be more than you can manage in your older years.

Once you've worked out your *debt free strategy*, plan out how long it will take to pay off the first bill, then the next bill, with all the money continuing to roll down the list against all the bills. Record the date that each bill will be gone in column 6 on the *Bill Payoff Order* form from Appendix A.

You should continue to track your progress every month against the *Bill Payoff Order* schedule. This will help you to avoid wasting money on nonessentials, while you're paying off bills. If you know when a bill is supposed to be paid off, and it's not, you know you have been undisciplined in sticking to your plan. And you know how far off schedule you are. Remember, our goal is not to fool ourselves into thinking that we are addressing the problem, it is to get the job done! Assuming you follow your payoff plan, you will soon be able to say "*Good-bye*" to credit ratings, and all the humiliation that go with credit.

Don't let yourself slip into the negative emotional trap that "*this is some kind of super-restrictive budget.*" This is not a *budget;* it is a *resource management plan* that simply guides you on how to best use your financial resources. It is not a restrictive approach to using money, but it is an approach to building a future. Most importantly, it will make you "Un-vulnerable," and eventually, rich.

CHAPTER 6

OPERATE ON A CASH BASIS

After paying off your debts, you'll began investing what had been going to debt-elimination. You'll be your own bank, your own credit card company, and you will never need to use the banks and the credit card companies again.

We've been trained to believe in credit, in fact, we've been brainwashed that we can't live without it. We are told to get and keep a good credit rating. Why? So, we can get more credit. But credit isn't your friend. You may need to buy your first home on credit. But that can also be accomplished without credit if you have enough patience.

When someone offers you credit, they're not giving you anything. If they offer you a $2,500 Visa card, they're not giving you $2,500. They are merely moving up the date at which you can spend money that you'll need to earn and pay back. They also charge you a high interest rate, which is additional money that you must earn.

Credit takes more money away from you than the actual value of the thing you buy on credit. The extra money you are giving to the credit company is money that you should be investing in your future. You are giving away your future retirement wealth just to have a few extra things now. The actual cost of using credit is greater than you think. You'll wake up one day wanting to stop working, only to realize that you can't. But it doesn't have to be that way, once you break the credit addiction, you are free to operate on a cash basis, and invest thousands towards your retirement.

A benefit of operating on cash even before you pay off your mortgage is, you've paid off your charge card, you begin paying off your mortgage balance by adding in all the dollars that use to be wasted on credit card payments. Then one day the kitchen stove breaks. Most people would get it repaired by using a credit card, but you'll take the money you were going to add to your mortgage payment that month and use it to pay cash to repair or buy a new kitchen stove.

Now you've paid off your mortgage and you're putting all the money that used to be wasted on credit card debt and your mortgage payments into investments.

Then one day your car dies. Most people would go to the bank and apply for a car loan, but you just hold off on your investments for one month and buy a used car for cash. Or, if necessary, you pull a little out of your liquid investment account and buy a better car, with cash.

Impulse buying is one of the most wealth-draining habits Americans do. It's quite easy, to flop down a credit card to pay for it. But it's much harder to spend cash on something you don't really need than it was to just whip out the credit card and buy it.

If you really need something, you can buy it with cash at this stage of your financial life. And that's what financial freedom is all about, you can enjoy each purchase without the pressure of having to pay for it for years into the future.

When you operate on cash, the process becomes its own buying controller. You will begin to think longer and harder about each purchase and be a lot less likely to buy things you really don't need.

CHAPTER 7

BEGAN BUILDING YOUR WEALTH

After paying off all your debts, both credit accounts and home mortgage, you then want to take the same amount you were paying on all the bills and focus on wealth-building investments.

Something unexpected might come up, so you should start the wealth-building process by putting about a half years' worth of required income into a liquid (easily convertible to cash) account such as a money market account or an assets management account, like a Schwab One account. This is so you can easily withdraw any amount you might need in case of an emergency.

A *Schwab one* account lets you deposit money, then write checks against that money just like a bank. But the account is also a one-stop brokerage and portfolio management account for making and managing all your investments.

The Debt Free Strategy is based on the premise that you do not want to deal with a lot of complexities when investing for your retirement wealth. You don't want to have to transact with each mutual fund company individually. A *Schwab One* account offers many popular mutual funds at zero commission. Of course, there are other brokerage companies that offer similar services. Whatever type of account you choose for your emergency cash fund make sure that it is both interest-bearing and liquid (easily withdrawn).

Next, you will begin to invest your money each month into less liquid but higher-growth investments. Many people recommend that you invest in mutual funds. These can be stock funds, bond funds or other types of investments that are managed by professionals with a proven track record. Experts, recommend that you do not do your own individual-stock investing. Nonprofessional investors usually don't come out ahead of the professional mutual fund managers.

The main reason I recommend mutual funds is that they give you the benefits you should be looking for in your investing strategy. Remember, one of the main concepts behind *the Debt Free Strategy* is "Simplicity and Safety." Mutual fund investing is simple and quite a bit safer than investing in individual securities yourself.

They may not always offer you the biggest gains available, but they will offer you a solid return potential, while giving you considerable protection against crashing.

Mutual funds will provide you with wealth-building power, while freeing you from having to personally research each individual company or security that you might consider investing in. Mutual funds are just what they sound like, a fund created by people "mutually" pooling their money for the purpose of investing.

The people who pooled their money and bought shares in the fund are the "Owners" of a company (the fund). Their company invests in other companies, government debt instruments, money markets and the like. The owners of this investing company (the shareholders in the mutual fund) then participate in the profits or losses from these investments, proportionately to their number of shares in the fund. Mutual fund shareholders include individuals like you and me, as well as institutions such as banks, insurance companies and pension funds.

An advantage of putting your money into mutual funds is that they automatically give you diversification, something that is crucial to protecting your assets. Mutual funds invest in a variety of stocks, bonds, or other securities, and therefore are insulated from being devasted by a drop in one single investment.

Mutual funds, fits in with our *Debt Free Strategy*, because the fund manager is minding the store for you, so you can relax while your assets are growing in value. That makes mutual funds the perfect investment for your retirement.

You can't beat the money-growing power of the U.S. stock market. The stock market is a powerful wealth-building tool, and you should be investing in it. But realize the market and the value of your shares will sometimes drop dramatically. This is normal and to be expected. When it happens, ignore the drops, and buy more shares. When you can live on 4% of your investments per year, you are financially independent. If you invest 12,000 a year you could easily grow that to more than a million over time.

Many people have 401(k) plans at work. The 401(k) is a great retirement investment plan, because you're earning around 50% on your money just from your employer's contribution alone.

Plus, the growth of the total investment accumulates tax-deferred until you begin taking distributions in retirement.

When considering investments, you should also consider the effects of taxes on the growth of your investments. There are three kinds of investments when it comes to this issue: tax-free, tax-deferred, and non-tax-deferred.

Tax-free investments are usually debt obligations of a governmental body. The most popular are tax-free municipal bonds. They are free from federal income taxes, and in some states, they are free of state income taxes as well (called double tax-free). These investments yield lower returns than taxable investments, but you must consider the value of not having to pay the taxes on your growth.

Tax-deferred investments let the interest accumulate in your account without your having to pay current taxes on the interest income or capital gains. The most common forms of tax-deferred investment plan are the Individual Retirement Account (IRA), the Keogh (for self-employed) and the 401(k) plans offered by many employers.

A tax-deferred plan should be a part of your investment strategy because the increased value of having the full interest compound each month is unbelievable. It can make a difference of hundreds of thousands of dollars in your future wealth. Tax-deferred investments usually come with tax penalty if you pull the money out before your retirement.

The idea behind these types of investment products is that, when you begin withdrawing the money later in life, you will be in a lower income bracket. The income taxes on non-tax-deferred investments must be paid in the tax year the gain is realized.

Throughout the building wealth stage of your Debt Free plan, you will, of course, maintain the necessary insurance to cover you from catastrophic occurrences.

CHAPTER 8

WHEN WILL YOU BE DEBT-FREE?

To get an idea of how long it takes you to get completely out of debt, including your mortgage, we will use the Debt Free Calculator form in Appendix B. First total up all your debt balances, including your mortgage balance. This will be a substantial number, but you should be encouraged when you see what happens as you short-circuit the impact of compound interest, by paying these bills off by the shortest amount of time.

Next total up all your monthly net income. Forget about what was going into savings because you are going to stop saving for now. You want to get as much monthly income working on the pay-down as possible. Your money will do you a lot better paying off 20% debt load than it will earning 5%, 6%, or 8% in savings.

Locate your approximate total debt amount in the Total Debt Amount column, along the left edge of the Debt Free Calculator chart in Appendix B. Then run your finger across to the right until you reach your approximate total monthly amount available for paying on all your bills, including your mortgage.

This income amount should include both your *Rocket Booster* and the normal minimum monthly payments on all your bills, but not the money that will go towards non-debt, monthly expenses like food, utilities, gasoline, and insurance.

When you've located this monthly amount, follow the column up to the line at the top of the table and you will see the approximate number of years it will take you to get completely out of debt.

This chart demonstrates why you want to put the most you

can into your monthly payoff *Rocket Booster*. The lower the monthly amount you pay against your total credit debt load, the longer it will take you to pay it off.

If your debt, including your mortgage, totaled $100,000, and the total monthly income (including all *Rocket Booster* amounts) you had available for paying on your debt was $2,500, you would first locate $100,000 in the left-most column, then look across to the right and find "2536".

This is the amount closest to the $2,500 you have available each month. Then run you finger up to the top of that column and your answer is 4 years! All your debts, including your home, would be paid off in just 4 years.

To think on how brief of time that is, simply think back four years ago. That's how quickly you could be looking back and recalling how hard it was to carry your heavy debt load. For the first time in your life, you will be able to make your own choices.

No boss will be able to hold a job over your head because you won't go bankrupt if you lose your job. You could easily live on savings until you found other work, or you could even work at McDonald's if you had to, and still be ok. The important thing is that the pressure would be off, and you'd have options.

Think about the anxiety people have over the economy, or their company's stability. When layoffs begin people panic because they know that they can't survive without their paycheck each month. But when you have no debts, all you need to worry about is eating, heating, and paying taxes. That takes a lot less money each month than you're spending now, so even a small savings account could sustain you for an extended amount of time.

CHAPTER 9

WHEN CAN YOU RETIRE?

To give you an example of how quickly your investments can add up, and how quickly you could retire on the interest income, see the *Wealth-Building/Retirement Calculator* in Appendix C. Find the approximate amount you will be investing each month, after all your debts are paid off. This amount should be the total of all of what used to be your monthly bill payments amounts, including your mortgage payment plus your initial *Rocket Booster*.

Now follow that line across to the number of years you plan to continue putting this amount into your investments. There you will find the approximate total amount that would be built up in your investment accounts, and after the dash you will see the approximate monthly interest payment or distribution you could receive from your investments, each month for the rest of your life.

Now that sounds like real financial independence to me. No bills, you own your home, and you have good money coming in every month, whether you work or not.

A quick look at the numbers on the chart shows that, if you were to maintain a strong monthly investment pattern, you could retire quite comfortably in as few as 5 years. That is reality, not the baloney you hear from all the get-rich schemes. And it certainly beats living on Social Security alone or working till the day you die.

You can also help those who need you. One of the major benefits of getting out of debt and on a cash, basis is that you are then able to help the people in your life who really need it. Whether it's an aging parent, a sibling in trouble, or starving children around the world...you will have the resources to help. Most people want to help others, but they get frustrated when they can hardly take care of their own needs. By following the Debt Free and wealth-building strategy, you can quickly get to a point where you have the option to share as much of your wealth as you, want.

You really can't take it with you, but you don't have to leave all your wealth in the hands of Banks, Insurance Companies, Credit Card Companies, and Mortgage Companies. You should decide how much of your wealth you want to spend on yourself, how much you want to leave behind, and to whom it should go to.

Following the Debt Free Strategy will get you to that point in the shortest possible amount of time.

If you get any criticism for taking a radically different financial path, remember that 96% of the people in this country do not ever achieve financial freedom or independence (IRS study), so if you look around you at how other people are managing their finances... and do the exact opposite...you have a 96% chance of being right! You are beginning the process of becoming truly financially free. As you continue this exciting transformation of your life, wouldn't today be the perfect day to start.

(Keep your feet on the ground but keep reaching for the stars.) Radio personality (Casey Kasen) would end each broadcast with that statement. I've always tried to live by that statement, and it's inspired me to produce my own statement, "Think and Grow rich."

Thank you for reading this book. I hope it has provided you some insights into utilizing the power of money to work for you.

APPENDIX A

BILL PAY-OFF ORDER

Write down each debt in column 1, it's total balance in column 2, the bill's minimum monthly payment in column 3, then divide the total balance by the monthly payment, putting the answer in column 4. Prioritize pay-off starting with lowest division answer as the first bill to pay off, putting the answer in column 5 and the projected payoff date in column 6.

Name of Debt	Total Balance	Monthly Payment	Division Answer	Pay-Off Priority	Pay-Off Date
1	2	3	4	5	6

APPENDIX B

DEBT FREE CALCULATOR

Locate your total debt in the Total Debt Amount column, along the left edge of the chart. Then run your finger across to the right until you reach your total monthly amount available for paying on all your bills, including your mortgage. When you have located this monthly amount, follow the column up to the line at the top of the table and you will see the approximate number of years it will take you to get completely out of debt.

Total Debt Amount	1 yr.	2 yrs.	3 yrs.	4 yrs.	5 yrs.	6 yrs.	7 yrs.
$1,000.00	88	46	32	25	21	19	17
$3,000.00	264	138	97	76	64	56	50
$5,000.00	440	231	161	127	106	93	83
$7,000.00	615	323	226	178	149	130	116
$10,000.00	879	461	323	254	212	185	166
$15,000.00	1319	692	484	380	319	278	249
$20,000.00	1758	923	645	507	425	371	332
$30,000.00	2637	1384	968	761	637	556	498
$40,000.00	3517	1846	1291	1015	850	741	664
$50,000.00	4396	2307	1613	1268	1062	926	830
$75,000.00	6594	3461	2420	1902	1594	1389	1245
$100,000.00	8792	4614	3227	2536	2125	1853	1660
$125,000.00	10989	5768	4033	3170	2656	2316	2075
$150,000.00	13187	6922	4840	3804	3187	2779	2490
$200,000.00	17583	9229	6453	5073	4249	3705	3320
$250,000.00	21979	11536	8067	6341	5312	4631	4150
$300,000.00	26375	13843	9680	7609	6374	5558	4980

APPENDIX C

WEALTH-BUILDING/RETIREMENT CALCULATOR

Find the approximate amount you will be investing each month, after all your debts are paid off. This amount should be the total of all of what used to be your monthly bill payments amounts, including your mortgage payment plus your initial *Rocket Booster*.

Now follow that line across to the number of years you plan to continue putting this amount into your investments. There you will find the approximate total amount that would be built up in your investment accounts, and after the dash you will see the approximate monthly interest payment or distribution you could receive from your investments, each month for the rest of your life.

Monthly Investment Amount	5yrs.	10 yrs.	15 yrs.
$500.00	39,041 – 312/mo	103,276 – 826/mo	208,962 - 1,672/mo
$1,000.00	78,082 – 625/mo	206,552 - 1,652/mo	417,924 - 3,343/mo
$2,000.00	156,165 - 1,249/mo	413,104 - 3,305/mo	835,849 - 6,687/mo
$3,000.00	234,247 - 1,874/mo	619,656 - 4,957/mo	1,253,772 - 10,030/mo
$5,000.00	390,412 - 3,123/mo	1,032,760 - 8,262/mo	2,089,621 - 16,717/mo
$7,500.00	585,618 - 4,685/mo	1,549,140 - 12,393/mo	3,134,431 - 25,075/mo

THE END

Thank you for taking the time to read "How to become Debt Free," if you enjoyed it, please consider telling your friends or posting a review. Word of mouth is an author's best friend and very much appreciated.

    www.amazon.com/author/rickycorumbooks

    Thank you, *Ricky Corum*